Income Shifting Your Life: A Greenprint for Achieving Financial Abundance

Written by Elsun Gunter

Table Of Contents

Chapter 1: Understanding Financial Abundance

Chapter 2: Evaluating Your Current Financial Situation

Chapter 3: Setting Financial Goals

Chapter 4: Budgeting and Money Management

Chapter 5: Building Multiple Streams of Income

Chapter 6: Planning for Retirement

Chapter 7: Building and Protecting Wealth

Chapter 8: Cultivating a Growth Mindset

Chapter 9: Staying Motivated and on Track

Conclusion

Chapter 1: Understanding Financial Abundance

Financial abundance refers to a state of having more than enough money to meet your needs and desires. It's a state where you are not worried about money and can afford the things you want in life, both now and in the future. Achieving financial abundance requires a combination of smart financial planning, hard work, and being intentional with your money. It's important to understand your income, expenses, and savings to create a budget and make informed decisions about spending, investing, and saving money. Having financial abundance also means having a positive attitude towards money and viewing it as a tool to help you achieve your goals and live a fulfilling life, rather than as a source of stress or anxiety. Cultivating a mindset of abundance and gratitude can help you attract more abundance into your life. Ultimately, financial abundance is about having control over your finances, feeling secure about your financial future, and having the freedom to make choices that align with your values and goals. Financial abundance is important for several reasons:

Financial Security: Having financial abundance means having a cushion of savings and assets that can provide a sense of security and stability, even in the face of unexpected events like job loss, illness, or emergencies.

Freedom of Choice: Financial abundance provides the freedom to make choices about how you spend your time and money, without worrying about making ends meet. This can lead to a greater sense of happiness and fulfillment.

Ability to Pursue Passions and Interests: Financial abundance can provide the resources needed to pursue hobbies, interests, and passions, whether that means traveling, volunteering, or starting a business.

Reduced Stress and Anxiety: Financial stress is a major source of anxiety for many people, and financial abundance can help reduce this stress and allow you to focus on other aspects of your life.

Improved Relationships: Money is often a source of tension in relationships, and financial abundance can help eliminate these tensions and improve relationships with loved ones.

Legacy Building: Financial abundance can also allow you to build a legacy, by providing resources for your family, supporting causes you care about, and leaving a lasting impact on the world. Overall, financial abundance is important because it provides the foundation for a happy, fulfilling, and meaningful life, free from financial stress and worry.

The relationship between mindset and financial abundance is a close one. Your mindset, or the way you think and feel about money, can have a big impact on your financial well-being and your ability to attract and maintain financial abundance. For example, if you have a scarcity mindset, you may view money as a finite resource, and focus on avoiding debt, cutting expenses, and hoarding your money. On the other hand, if you have a mindset of abundance, you may view money as a tool to help you achieve your goals, and focus on generating income, investing, and giving back. A positive and abundant mindset can help you make better financial decisions and create a more prosperous life. It can also help you overcome financial setbacks and challenges, and increase your resilience in the face of financial stress. Some ways to cultivate an abundant mindset include practicing gratitude, setting clear financial goals, and visualizing financial success. Surrounding yourself with positive influences, such as books, podcasts, and people who have a successful financial mindset can also help. Conclusively, a growth-oriented, abundant mindset can help you create the financial future you want, and attract the abundance and prosperity you desire.

Chapter 2: Evaluating Your Current Financial Situation & Understanding your income and expenses

Understanding your income and expenses is an important step in managing your finances and achieving financial abundance. It involves tracking all the money you earn (income) and spend (expenses) over a period of time.

Here are some steps to help you understand your income and expenses:

1. Gather financial information: Collect all your recent bank and credit card statements, bills, receipts, and any other documentation that shows your income and expenses.

2. Categorize your income and expenses: Divide your income and expenses into categories, such as housing, food, transportation, entertainment, etc. This will help you see where your money is going and identify areas where you might be overspending.

3. Track your spending: Keep track of your spending for a set period of time, such as a week or a month. You can do this manually or use a budgeting app or software.

4. Analyze your results: After tracking your income and expenses, review the information to see where your money is going. Look for patterns and areas where

you can reduce spending, or increase income.

5. Create a budget: Based on your income and expenses, create a budget that allows you to live within your means, save money, and reach your financial goals.

By understanding your income and expenses, you can gain control over your finances, make informed decisions about spending and saving, and work towards financial abundance.

Identifying areas for improvement is a critical step in achieving financial abundance. It involves reviewing your financial situation and identifying areas where you can make changes to improve your financial health.

Here are some steps to help you identify areas for improvement:

6. Review your income and expenses: Look at your budget and spending habits to see if you can reduce expenses or increase income.

7. Evaluate your debt: Look at your debts and determine if you can pay them off faster or if there are better options for managing the debt.

8. Evaluate your savings: Look at your savings and determine if you're saving enough to reach your financial goals, or if you need to increase your savings rate.

9. Evaluate your investments: Look at your investments and determine if they align with your financial goals, and if they are diversified and managed appropriately.

10. Evaluate your insurance: Look at your insurance coverage and determine if it's adequate and if there are any changes you can make to better protect your finances.

By identifying areas for improvement and making changes, you can take control of your finances and work towards financial abundance. Don't be discouraged if you find areas for improvement, it's a normal part of the process, and with the right plan and action, you can overcome any obstacles and reach your financial goals.

Chapter 3: Setting Financial Goals

Setting financial goals is an important aspect of managing your finances and achieving financial stability. Here's a comparison between short-term and long-term financial goals:

Short-term financial goals:

- Building an emergency fund
- Paying off high-interest debt such as credit card balances or personal loans
- Creating a budget and sticking to it

- Saving for a specific short-term purchase or expense, such as a down payment on a car or a trip

Long-term financial goals:

- Building a retirement fund and planning for a secure retirement
- Paying off a mortgage or other long-term debt
- Investing in stocks, bonds, or other financial instruments to grow wealth
- Establishing a financial plan for the future, including savings and investment strategies, insurance coverage, and estate planning

When setting financial goals, it's important to consider both short-term and long-term goals. Short-term goals can help you make progress and achieve quick wins, while long-term goals can help you establish a solid financial foundation for the future. Additionally, it's important to make your goals specific, measurable, attainable, relevant, and time-bound (SMART goals). This will help you stay motivated and focused as you work towards achieving your financial goals. Setting goals is a fundamental part of personal and professional success. However, not all goals are created equal. SMART goals provide a framework for setting and achieving your dreams, by ensuring that they are specific, measurable, achievable, relevant, and time-bound. SMART goals are a powerful tool for setting and achieving your aspirations. This acronym stands for Specific, Measurable, Achievable, Relevant, and Time-bound. Each of these components is essential in ensuring that your goals are focused, actionable, and attainable. SMART goals provide a roadmap for success, and there are numerous benefits to using this framework. By setting SMART goals, you increase the likelihood of reaching your aspirations, you can track your progress, and you can adjust your strategy as needed. Setting SMART goals is just the first step. The real challenge is staying motivated and on track. No journey is without obstacles, and the journey to achieving your goals is no exception.

In today's fast-paced world, it is easy to get caught up in the pursuit of financial success. However, it is essential to understand that there is more to life than just money. A fulfilling life requires a balance between financial stability and personal satisfaction. Financial stability is crucial for a happy and secure life. While financial stability is important, it is not the only factor that contributes to a fulfilling life. Achieving a balance between financial and non-financial goals requires a thoughtful approach. As with any goal, there will be obstacles along the way.

Finally, it is important to take the time to celebrate your successes, both financial and non-financial. Achieving a balance between financial and non-financial goals is essential for a fulfilling life. By setting and working towards both types of goals, you can create a life that is not only financially secure but also personally satisfying.

Chapter 4: Budgeting and Money Management

Budgeting and money management are critical skills that are necessary for financial stability and independence. A budget is essentially a plan for how you will allocate your income and expenses over a specified period of time. By creating a budget and following it, you can take control of your finances, reduce debt, maximize savings, and achieve your financial goals. In this guide, we will discuss the importance of creating a budget, techniques for tracking expenses and sticking to a budget, and strategies for reducing debt and maximizing savings.

Creating a budget is one of the most effective ways to take control of your finances. A budget helps you understand how much money you have coming in and going out, so you can make informed decisions about how to allocate your resources. With a budget, you can:

- Track your spending: A budget allows you to see exactly where your money is going, so you can identify areas where you may be overspending or areas where you can cut back.

- Set financial goals: Whether you want to save for a down payment on a house, pay off debt, or build an emergency fund, a budget can help you set financial goals and track your progress towards achieving them.

- Manage debt: A budget can help you prioritize paying off debt, so you can become debt-free as soon as possible.

- Maximize savings: By tracking your spending and allocating money towards savings, you can build an emergency fund and save for long-term goals, like retirement.

Once you've created a budget, it's essential to stick to it. Here are some techniques you can use to help you track your expenses and stick to your budget:

- Use budgeting software or apps: There are many budgeting software and apps available that can help you track your expenses and stay on top of your budget.

- Write down all of your expenses: Keeping a written record of all of your expenses, no matter how small, can help you see where your money is going and make adjustments as needed.

- Avoid impulse purchases: Impulse purchases can quickly add up and blow your budget. To avoid impulse purchases, make a list of what you need before you go shopping and stick to it.

- Use cash instead of credit: When you use cash, you're more mindful of your spending because you can physically see the money leaving your wallet.

Reducing debt and maximizing savings are critical components of budgeting and money management. Here are some strategies for reducing debt and maximizing savings:

- Pay off high-interest debt first: High-interest debt, like credit card debt, can be expensive and take years to pay off. By paying off high-interest debt first, you can save money on interest charges and become debt-free faster.

- Create an emergency fund: An emergency fund is a savings account specifically for unexpected expenses. By having an emergency fund, you can avoid using credit cards or taking out loans when unexpected expenses arise.

- Save for long-term goals: In addition to an emergency fund, it's important to save for long-term goals like retirement. The earlier you start saving, the more time your money has to grow.

- Automate your savings: Setting up automatic savings transfers from your checking account to your savings account can help you save without having to think about it.

In conclusion, budgeting and money management are essential skills that can help you take control of your finances, reduce debt, maximize savings, and achieve your financial goals

Chapter 5: Building Multiple Streams of Income

Having multiple streams of income is an important aspect of financial stability and independence. It allows you to diversify your income sources, reduce your financial risk, and increase your earning potential. In this guide, we will discuss the importance of building multiple streams of income and explore some common ways to do so, including understanding passive income, investing in stocks, bonds, and real estate, and starting a side business. Passive income is a type of income that is earned with little or no ongoing effort. Examples of passive income include rental income from real estate, dividends from stocks, and royalties from intellectual property. Passive income can help you build wealth over time and provide you with a stable source of income. Investing in stocks, bonds, and real estate are all common ways to build multiple streams of income. Investing in stocks can help you earn dividends and potentially benefit from capital gains. Bonds offer a fixed rate of return and can provide a steady stream of income. Investing in real estate, whether through rental properties or real estate investment trusts (REITs), can provide you with passive rental income. Starting a side business is another way to build multiple streams of income. A side business can provide you with additional income and help you achieve financial independence. Some popular side businesses include freelance work, selling products online, and providing services like pet-sitting or home cleaning. Building multiple streams of income is an important aspect of financial stability and independence. By understanding passive income, investing in stocks, bonds, and real estate, and starting a side business, you can diversify your income sources, reduce your financial risk, and increase your earning potential.

Chapter 6: Planning for Retirement

Planning for retirement is a crucial aspect of financial planning that ensures that you have sufficient resources to support yourself during your retirement years. In this guide, we will discuss the importance of planning for retirement and explore the different types of retirement accounts, the process of creating a retirement plan, and how to maximize your Social Security benefits. There are several types of retirement accounts available to help you save for retirement, including traditional and Roth IRAs, 401(k) plans, and pension plans. Each type of account offers different tax benefits, contribution limits, and withdrawal rules, so it's important to understand the pros and cons of each option and choose the one that's right for you.

Creating a retirement plan involves assessing your current financial situation, setting retirement goals, and determining how much you need to save to reach those goals. It's also important to regularly review and adjust your plan as your financial situation changes. A retirement plan should include contributions to a retirement account, investment strategy, and a plan for managing debt and expenses. Social Security is an important source of retirement income for many people, and maximizing your benefits can help ensure that you have enough income to support yourself during retirement. This can be done by understanding the eligibility requirements, the calculation of benefits, and the strategies for claiming benefits, such as claiming early or delaying the claim to increase your monthly benefit. Planning for retirement is an important aspect of financial planning that helps ensure that you have sufficient resources to support yourself during your retirement years. By understanding the different types of retirement accounts, creating a retirement plan, and maximizing your Social Security benefits, you can feel confident and prepared for your future.

Chapter 7: Building and Protecting Wealth

Building and protecting wealth is an important aspect of financial planning that can help ensure a stable financial future. Wealth building involves increasing your assets and reducing your liabilities over time to reach financial independence and security. This can be done through smart investments, reducing debt, and increasing your income. Building wealth can help provide financial stability and independence, allowing you to achieve your financial goals and live the life you want. Minimizing taxes and protecting assets are important components of wealth building. This can be done by understanding the tax implications of your financial decisions and taking steps to reduce your tax burden, such as contributing to a retirement account or investing in a tax-advantaged account. Protecting your assets involves reducing the risk of financial loss, such as by diversifying your investments and purchasing insurance. Developing a wealth-building strategy involves setting financial goals, assessing your current financial situation, and determining the best steps to reach your goals. This can include creating a budget, reducing debt, increasing your income, and investing in stocks, bonds, or real estate. A wealth-building strategy should also include a plan for protecting your assets and minimizing taxes. Building and protecting wealth is an important aspect of financial planning that can help ensure a stable financial future. By understanding the concept of wealth building, minimizing taxes and protecting assets, and developing a wealth-building strategy, you can take control of your financial future and achieve financial independence and security.

Chapter 8: Cultivating a Growth Mindset

Cultivating a growth mindset is a crucial aspect of personal and financial growth. Your mindset has a significant impact on your financial success, and a growth mindset can help you overcome challenges and achieve financial abundance. In this chapter, we will discuss the importance of the power of the mind in achieving financial abundance, strategies for developing a growth mindset, and overcoming limiting beliefs and fear.

The power of the mind is a significant factor in achieving financial abundance. A growth mindset can help you overcome challenges and see opportunities, while a fixed mindset can limit your ability to achieve financial success. A growth mindset involves having a positive attitude towards growth and learning, being open to new ideas, and being resilient in the face of setbacks. Developing a growth mindset requires a commitment to personal growth and a willingness to learn and improve. Strategies for developing a growth mindset include:

- Setting clear and specific goals
- Seeking feedback and learning from mistakes
- Focusing on progress and not perfection
- Surrounding yourself with positive and supportive people
- Challenging yourself with new experiences and opportunities

Limiting beliefs and fear can hold you back from achieving financial abundance. Overcoming these obstacles requires recognizing and challenging negative thoughts and beliefs, and developing a positive mindset. This can be done by practicing gratitude, visualizing success, and seeking out opportunities for personal growth and learning. Cultivating a growth mindset is an important aspect of personal and financial growth. By understanding the power of the mind in achieving financial abundance, developing strategies for a growth mindset, and overcoming limiting beliefs and fear, you can increase your chances of financial success and achieve financial abundance.

Chapter 9: Staying Motivated and on Track

Staying motivated and on track is crucial for achieving your financial goals and maintaining financial stability. In this guide, we will discuss the importance of accountability and support, staying motivated through ups and downs, and celebrating successes and learning from failure. Accountability and support are essential elements in staying motivated and on track. Having a support system, such as a trusted friend or family member, can provide encouragement and accountability, helping you stay focused on your goals. Joining a financial support group or working with a financial advisor can also provide accountability and support. Staying motivated can be challenging, especially during times of uncertainty or financial setbacks. It is important to maintain a positive mindset and focus on the long-term goals, rather than short-term setbacks. Setting small, achievable goals can help maintain momentum and a sense of accomplishment. It is also helpful to celebrate small victories and take time to reflect on your progress. Celebrating successes and learning from failure are key components of staying motivated and on track. Celebrating successes, no matter how small, can help maintain a positive mindset and provide motivation to continue working towards your goals. Learning from failure can provide valuable lessons and insights, helping you make adjustments and improve your financial strategies. Staying motivated and on track is crucial for achieving financial stability and success. The importance of accountability and support, staying motivated through ups and downs, and celebrating successes and learning from failure, can help you maintain motivation and reach your financial goals.

Conclusion

Financial Abundance is a Journey, Not a Destination. Financial abundance is not a one-time event, but rather a continuous journey towards financial freedom. By understanding the principles of financial management, setting goals, and developing a growth mindset, anyone can work towards financial abundance and live a life of financial freedom. The principles of financial management are the foundation for achieving financial abundance. These principles include budgeting, saving, investing, and managing debt. Understanding these principles and applying them to your financial life can help you reach your financial goals and live a life of financial freedom. Setting clear and specific financial goals is essential for achieving financial abundance. Goals can range from short-term, such as paying off debt or building an emergency fund, to long-term, such as saving for retirement or buying a home. Setting goals provides a roadmap to financial freedom and helps you stay focused and motivated. Developing a growth mindset is key to achieving financial abundance. A growth mindset involves having a positive attitude towards growth and learning, being open to new ideas, and being resilient in the face of setbacks. Cultivating a growth mindset can help you overcome challenges and see opportunities, and is essential for financial success.

In conclusion, financial abundance is a journey, not a destination. By understanding the principles of financial management, setting goals, and developing a growth mindset, anyone can work towards financial abundance and live a life of financial freedom. With dedication, discipline, and a commitment to personal growth, financial freedom is within reach.

FOLLOW ME ON INSTAGRAM:
@INCOMESHIFTINGYOURLIFE

INCOMESHIFTINGYOURLIFE.COM

www.ingramcontent.com/pod-product-compliance
Lightning Source LLC
Chambersburg PA
CBHW072302170526
45158CB00003BA/1148